YOU KNOW YOU'RE A **CHILD** OF THE

90s

WHEN...

Helen Lincoln

summersdale

YOU KNOW YOU'RE A CHILD OF THE 90s WHEN...

Summersdale Publishers Ltd

46 West Street

Chichester

West Sussex

PO19 1RP

UK

www.summersdale.com

Printed and bound in China

ISBN: 978-1-84953-164-1

Substantial discounts on bulk quantities of Summersdale books are available to corporations, professional associations and other organisations. For details contact Summersdale Publishers by telephone: +44 (0) 1243 771107, fax: +44 (0) 1243 786300 or email: nicky@summersdale.com.

To...Lauren...........................

With love

From.........Nan...............

x x x

You know you're a child of the 90s when...

You can remember Harry Potter before his voice broke.

The words 'Gareth Southgate' and 'penalties' still make you angry.

You always get the irresistible urge to re-enact the iconic prow scene in *Titanic* whenever you find yourself on a ferry.

You still believe, in all honesty, that you are Bridget Jones.

Dolly the Sheep and BSE made you into a staunch vegetarian.

You still make mix tapes for your friends of music you know they'll love, and you're slightly suspicious of MP3s.

You feel intensely grateful that Facebook and mobile phones with video recorders didn't exist while you were learning how to party.

Your idea of dancing was mooching about in a long jumper while looking at the floor.

You're still not sure who killed Laura Palmer, and you've always wanted to go to a diner and order a slice of cherry pie and a 'damn fine cup of coffee'.

You can get a guaranteed laugh from your friends by saying 'Eranu' in a silly voice, or offering a cup of tea with the words 'Go on, go on, go on, go on...' in your best Irish accent.

You're still getting to grips with Damien Hirst's seminal piece *The Physical Impossibility of Death in the Mind of Someone Living*, and it's the reason you've been having nightmares about sharks ever since.

Your role model was Ally McBeal, not for her high-flying career but because of her enormous pout.

You were the first to wear coloured contact lenses when they came out, even though the sight of you made small children cry.

Your parents' shed is still crammed with tinned food and foil blankets in preparation for nuclear war due to the complications surrounding the Millennium Bug.

You wished your parents
were Ma and Pop Larkin –
then everything would
be 'Perfick!'

You sported the 'Rachel' cut, as did all your friends.

You can remember being
told off by your parents
for saying 'Eat my shorts!'
to your grandma.

You always wanted to be
Mr Black in your gang of
mates, but somehow you
always ended up as
Mr Pink.

After watching *Four Weddings and a Funeral* when it first came out, you thought all men would be like Hugh Grant until you started dating.

You feel a certain nostalgia for obvious shop names like Sock Shop, Tie Rack and Knickerbox – where did they all go?

You can remember saving up your pocket money to buy a pair of Spice Girls-style chunky-heeled shoes. But instead of looking cool, you looked like you had two club feet.

You were an outcast for
months at school after
your mum wouldn't let
you go grunge on
non-uniform day.

You still check under the
bed for Gremlins before
going to sleep.

You still have a thing for Pierce Brosnan – even though you have to admit that his Bond was a bit naff.

You haven't lived down the time when your mates convinced you to ask the lady at the Boots counter for some *Fight Club* soap.

Your parents let you redecorate your bedroom after being inspired by *Changing Rooms* – and it ended up looking like a tart's boudoir, of course.

You desperately wanted to pass your driving test so that you and your mates could re-enact the 'Bohemian Rhapsody' head-banging scene in *Wayne's World.*

You remember having your first email account and being really excited about getting emails – even the ones that just said 'Message Undeliverable'.

You can't think of a single Shakespeare play without an image of Kenneth Branagh popping into your head.

You learned Morse code because someone told you once that the killer's name is revealed in the pips at the start of each *Inspector Morse* episode.

You have a crystal on the dashboard of your car, believing that it will help you drive better.

Staying at your parents' timeshare apartment in Benidorm felt like the height of sophistication, and you used to brag about it to your mates.

You quizzed the careers officer at school about qualifications required to be a pet detective after watching *Ace Ventura*.

You wouldn't consider going out without squirting yourself all over with CK One.

You remember what you were doing the moment you heard Take That had split up.

You only agreed to go on a date with the boy next door because he had tickets to see Oasis.

You can bore for Britain
on the relative merits of
the old and new versions
of *Star Wars*.

You still have the nickname 'Streaky' due to the badly applied fake tan you used to slap on before school.

You have a collection of over a hundred scrunchies that you can't bring yourself to chuck away.

The ultimate must-have household appliance when you were growing up was a dishwasher – and you're still waiting for one!

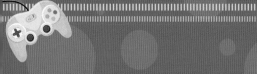

You have fond memories of singing 'Gillette, the best a man can get!' to your brother after he incurred his first shaving injury.

You have an irresistible urge to shout 'Nicole!' when you see a woman driving a Renault Clio, and 'Papa!' when it's a man.

You're still wondering why Madonna named her daughter after a cricket ground.

You still get the urge to say 'NOT!' at the end of every sentence.

You borrowed your dad's Handycam to make your own version of *The Blair Witch Project*.

You laughed your head off when someone told you we'd win the Ashes in Australia one day.

You still talk about 'videos', even though you only have DVDs now, and you still 'video' programmes on your TV set-top box.

You used to wear
stick-on earrings.

You never could get to
grips with those Magic
Eye pictures but you
never let on.

You experimented with
dying your hair blonde
and styling it into a 'flick'
at the front.

You remember having heated 'Oasis vs Blur' debates with your friends.

You indulged in the see-
through, coloured plastic
dummy craze while
at school.

You thought having a pager was the height of modern technological advancement.

Mario Kart, *Street Fighter II* and *Doom* were (and still are) at the top of your videogame wish list.

You owned a yo-yo but never really mastered anything but the classic 'up-down, up-down' trick.

Bill and Ted, Beavis and Butthead and Thelma and Louise are some of your on-screen heroes.

You have fond memories of the phrases, 'Gladiators, rrready?', 'Tooo the Crystal Dome!' and 'It's good, but it's not the one.'

You thought Sweater Shop sweatshirts and Kickers moccasins were as cool as it gets.

Europe is where you go on holiday, rather than the place you live in.

You can remember going into the barber's and asking for an 'under cut'.

You still haven't got used to referring to a Marathon as a Snickers or Opal Fruits as Starburst.

Even after two decades, you still can't get your Tamagotchi to survive longer than two weeks.

You know what Pogs and Tazos are, but never quite figured out how to use them.

You know how to party
like it's 1999.

90210 just doesn't sound the same without *Beverly Hills* in front of it.

You were shocked
to discover *Northern
Exposure* wasn't filmed
in Alaska.

A moustache didn't look good on anyone, except Nigel Mansell.

You didn't see anything wrong with spending your Friday night watching *The Word.*

If someone mentions Gazza, you immediately think of a kebab.

You thought you were particularly smart when informing your friends that Hercule Poirot was Belgian and not French.

You felt cool reading *FHM*, even though you didn't know what the letters meant.

You used to think, 'Next year Tim Henman will win Wimbledon.'

You logically thought: the bigger the speakers, the louder the music.

**Batman and Robin means
Del Boy and Rodney.**

You can't get 'I'll be back'
out of your vocabulary.

You think the sound of monks singing doesn't quite work unless there's an electronic beat in the background.

You remember a time when you could take a penknife and a razor in your hand luggage and nobody in airport security would bat an eyelid.

You know all the words to 'Don't Look Back in Anger', but you still don't really know what the song's about.

You still think of anywhere in Eastern Europe as being somehow a 'new' holiday destination.

£2 coins still feel like an innovation, and the 5p, 10p and 50p coins still seem a bit too small.

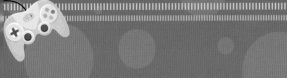

You remember feeling, in the middle of a spring night in 1997, that 'Things Can Only Get Better'.

You thought Manchester United's title supremacy wouldn't last much longer.

You remember telling your friends that *The Lord of the Rings* was too huge and epic to ever appear as a film.

You still respond to mild pieces of bad news with a humorous 'Do I not like that.'

You remember when wearing a shellsuit was totally unremarkable – and when wearing a turquoise shellsuit meant you'd had a New Age religious experience.

TV talent shows used
to last an hour on a
Saturday night, and
nobody really talked
about them.

You remember when Big Brother was just something scary in a George Orwell novel.

You're glad that giant headphones are cool again – you can get your old ones out of the attic!

You Know You're a Child of the 50s When...

Helen Lincoln

ISBN: 978-1-84953-160-3

£4.99

Hardback

You Know You're a Child of the 60s When...

Mark Leigh and Mike Lepine

ISBN: 978-1-84953-161-0

£4.99

Hardback

You Know You're a Child of the 70s When...

Mark Leigh and Mike Lepine

ISBN: 978-1-84953-162-7

£4.99

Hardback

You Know You're a Child of the 80s When...

Mark Leigh and Mike Lepine

ISBN: 978-1-84953-163-4

£4.99

Hardback